Better Riding

Lt.-Col. 'Bill' Froud, OBE, FBHS, the National Instructor to the British Horse Society.

Better Riding

by Lt.-Colonel 'Bill' Froud

The National Instructor to the British Horse Society

Written in collaboration with the British Horse Society

PHOTOGRAPHS BY PETER ROBERTS

KAYE & WARD LTD, LONDON
in association with
HICKS, SMITH & SONS, AUSTRALIA AND NEW ZEALAND

First published by
Kaye & Ward Limited
194-200 Bishopsgate, London EC2M 4PA
1971

ISBN 0 7182 0159 0

Printed in England by
Straker Brothers, Ltd, Bishopsgate
London, EC2M 4NT

Contents

The author and publishers would like to thank Miss Kate Crilley, Miss Tina Rose and Mr Paul Fielder for their help in producing many of the photographs in this book.

1. Introduction to riding

No longer is riding a sport only for the wealthy or for the person living in the country. Indeed, riding is becoming more of an urban sport than a country one in many parts of the world. And today there are more people, young and old, riding in the British Isles than ever before. This is due, of course, partly to more leisure hours and better general riding facilities.

Unfortunately, the vast majority of people who ride never get beyond a very elementary standard and therefore never capture the very real thrill of riding boldly across country, galloping round a point-to-point course, or taking part in the many equestrian activities and competitions that are available today.

I think this is due mainly to three reasons. Firstly, the majority of would-be riders do not make much genuine effort to study the characteristics and the mental processes of the horse. Naturally the novice rider is usually nervous and indecisive in his actions: the horse responds to this by being suspicious and unpredictable. Therefore a basis of mutual confidence must be established before riding ever starts. The novice rider *must* spare some time at this essential introductory phase.

Secondly, comparatively few riders will take the time and trouble to develop a well-balanced and effective seat. The trouble is that most people want to learn quickly, and this cannot be done. Most sports demand the co-ordination and development of mind *and* muscle, so that

No longer a sport only for the wealthy. This is a Pony Club scene.

certain actions become automatic reflexes. Never is this more the case than in riding.

The horse has a natural centre of gravity which changes according to the pace at which he is moving, or whether he is going up or down hill. It is the rider's first task to position himself in the saddle so that his centre of gravity is as closely aligned with the horse as possible. The rider's weight must never be dead weight; it must assist the horse's movements, not oppose it. When the horse moves, the rider's seat must be associated with this movement. It must be firm, yet supple. A rider who is stiff and rigid will set up stiffness and resistance in the horse. The seat must be independent of the reins. It must be athletic enough to stay in balance with the horse, yet allow complete freedom of the head and neck.

A rider without this firm and independent seat cannot clearly indicate his wishes to the horse; confusion and the use of force are the result. And when a rider resorts to force, he will inevitably be defeated, although he may have appeared to gain a temporary victory.

Basic faults in the seat stem from incorrect teaching in the first few lessons. Sometimes, of course, there are no lessons at all! And once muscles are incorrectly placed and used, it takes a great deal of hard work and concentration to eradicate the fault. The great French School at Saumur teaches riding in stages. The first is elementary equitation, the purpose being to develop the rider's seat on a trained horse, so that he may acquire sufficient ability to control his horse under normal circumstances, in the manège and across easy country; also that he may apply elementary aids smoothly, effectively and in harmony, producing a calm and generous response from his horse.

Notice the phrase 'develop the rider's seat on a trained horse'. Riding an untrained horse is the third reason why so many riders never progress beyond an elementary standard. The novice should learn to ride on a quiet, well-mannered horse that is obedient to the elementary aids, under the guidance of an experienced instructor. This is common sense even to

The rider's first task is to position himself in the saddle so that his centre of gravity is as closely aligned with the horse's as possible. This rider is in balance at the halt.

the least knowledgeable, but how often do we see fond parents buying 'green' three-year-olds for their learner children with disastrous results, both to horse and would-be riders!

CHARACTERISTICS OF THE HORSE

The experienced trainer and wise-thinking rider works with his horse's natural instincts and not against them. The horse's predominant instinct is to seek safety in flight: he will move away from pain or discomfort. In fact, he will anticipate the use of whip or spur and will move away before it is applied. We take advantage of this in his training.

The horse has limited intelligence and is highly suspicious of anything he doesn't understand. This instinct always requires the patience and understanding of the rider. For example, if your horse shies away from a strange object, it does more harm than good if you are rough with him or punish him. By doing this, you associate that particular object in his mind with punishment, and he will be even worse next time you approach it.

The horse is extremely gregarious and dislikes leaving the company of other horses, or his stable, the place he knows and trusts. This instinct can be used on occasion to the trainer's advantage, but over a period of time the horse must learn to obey the rider under all circumstances. The inexperienced rider must test his obedience in small things first and gradually increase the difficulty of the tests as obedience improves.

It is very largely due to the horse's excellent memory that we are able to train him at all. He rarely forgets anything he has been taught and unfortunately he will acquire bad habits just as quickly as good ones, so the rider must always proceed carefully and never allow a fault to occur without it being corrected. Once a bad habit becomes ingrained (and this can happen all too quickly) it is extremely difficult to eradicate. Good training is the acquisition of good habits, desired qualities, whereby you improve your horse. The final test of a good rider is this: does he improve the horse he rides?

The horse is very susceptible to reward. A soothing voice, a pat on the neck when he has done well, will associate an action with pleasant memory, and this is all part of the method of training. The feeding of titbits will encourage confidence, but should not be indulged in too liberally, otherwise the horse will become unmanageable and inclined to nip when the expected titbits are not forthcoming—I have seen pet ponies become quite vicious through over-petting. The horse has little or no reasoning power, however; he cannot relate cause and effect. If a horse is punished just one minute after doing something wrong, he doesn't connect the punishment with his wrongdoing. Confusion in his mind is the result. A horse should rarely be punished even by the most experienced trainer. Correction is the answer. If your horse wilfully disobeys, the action should be repeated immediately *at the same place* until obedience is achieved. The least sign of obedience must be rewarded.

The horse's sight and hearing are much more acute than ours, and a noise or sight that is commonplace to the rider can be a source of alarm to him. Watch your horse's ears; they work with his eyes and give a very good indication of his state of mind. By using his instincts to our advantage, by overcoming his fears, we gain his confidence. As he gains confidence in his rider, so he will learn to relax in his mind and in turn will relax his muscles, all of which will help to produce a more supple and amenable ride.

2. The seat

THE BEGINNER'S REFLEXES

A man on his feet has certain natural reflex actions that are quite wrong when we put him on a horse. Also his natural posture when standing or sitting is incorrect when he is placed in the saddle. Therefore, by constant thought and by exercise we must change the pedestrian's posture and reflexes into a horseman's. Here are the main examples of what I mean. Put a non-rider into the saddle and he will sit on it rather as he would on an armchair: weight back on his buttocks, legs forward, shoulders rounded and chest collapsed with the head thrust forward. Put his feet into the stirrup irons and he will push his feet against them with a stiff knee and ankle. These are sub-conscious reflexes. Put a rein in each hand and the reaction is to pull it.

To pull against a horse, however, is the beginning of the end; he is much stronger than any man and in a battle of pulling he will win, and will become a stronger and stronger puller.

Our first task, then, is to alter the rider's posture so that he may develop the right reflexes. The first and most important reflex action to remember and practise is 'the hand never pulls'. You overcome disobedience or pulling in the horse by *resisting* with the hand, and to do this successfully the hand must have a firm base to resist from, i.e. the body, which brings us back to the seat. I will refer to the hands again later.

When the horse moves, the rider's seat must be associated with his movements. In balance going up a hill.

POSITION

We have said in the first chapter that to ride well, with the minimum of effort from the rider and the least discomfort to the horse, the rider must sit 'in balance'. Looking at the skeleton of a horse, this position of 'balance' is to be found at the lowest part of the horse's back, just behind the withers. Here also the back is strongest, the ribs forming a fixed cage between backbone and breastbone. There must be no weight on the

Here the rider is sitting in a pulling attitude. The reins are too long, the knee and ankle are stiff, the lower leg is forward.

weaker part of the back—'the loins'—and the important dorsal muscles must be left free. In this position also, close to the withers, there is least movement, so the rider will find it easier for his body to conform to each pace.

THE SADDLE

To enable the rider to sit in exactly the right place he must first have a good central-position saddle that encourages him to sit deep into his horse. Most modern saddles are well made, but one occasionally still sees the type of saddle that slopes back towards the cantle, and the poor rider must climb a hill to sit in balance! When selecting a saddle the rider should ensure that the deepest part is well forward, and the waist narrow.

GRIP

The first few lessons in placing the rider in the saddle are vital, and the most destructive word to a good seat one can use is the word 'grip'. Tell a novice rider that he must grip with his knee and thigh (this is the most common expression) and the rider will stiffen the knee, turn his toe out and grip with the back of his calf and the large fleshy muscle of the thigh—upwards!—so that he squeezes himself out of the saddle like a cork out of a bottle, with his stirrup irons dangling without weight in them. Grip does play a part in producing the seat, but only when the right muscles have been developed. The seat is maintained by a combination of balance, suppleness, anticipation and adhesion.

IN BALANCE

First the rider's natural balance must be developed by placing him correctly in the saddle with the crotch well forward. The rider should feel weight on his seat bones, and not on the fleshy part of his buttocks. Some of the weight goes down to the thigh which runs downward and forward, the angle depending on the rider's conformation. The inside

A good general-purpose saddle that would encourage a rider to sit deep into his horse.

Gripping upwards with the back of the calf, the rider is forced out of the saddle like a cork out of a bottle.

Young riders practise a good thigh position with crossed stirrups.

The stirrups too short; the seat is cramped.

Here the stirrups are too long and the rider is tipping forward.

of the thigh lies softly against the saddle and in the early stages the knee will be away from the saddle; this does not matter.

If the knees are relaxed, the lower leg will come naturally back with the inside of the calf in contact with the horse's sides. The stirrup iron will be on the ball of the foot with the stirrup leather vertical. The length of the leather depends on the shape of the rider's thighs. A rider with a short thick thigh requires a proportionately shorter stirrup than does a person of equal height with a long thin thigh. Careful adjustment is essential; if leathers are too long the seat will be weakened by the rider tipping forward in an effort to reach them; if too short the knee will be cramped and the seat pushed to the rear of the saddle.

The ankle is a buffer; therefore it must not be locked, but to tension the muscles of the calf the heel must be just a little lower than the toe. The toe is at a natural angle, pointing forward and slightly out.

To be in balance the rider's body must be upright, with the shoulders open, his neck touching the back of his collar and his eyes looking forward. The head is very important to both balance and suppleness. If carried to one side or thrust forward it upsets the rider's balance and also causes him to stiffen on one side. To be balanced on your feet, or on a horse, your heel must be under your shoulder and one should see a straight line, shoulder-hip-heel. If your heel is in front of this line you will be behind the movement of the horse, if behind this line, in front of the movement.

The body must be straight but ready to conform with the horse's movement. The rider should sit in the saddle as though he is standing with knees bent and apart, ankles flexed, knees soft and hips supple. In this position the muscles of the thighs in particular will gradually strengthen and develop. After a few months of working at this position the seat will deepen and the rider will be able to adhere to the saddle with the whole of his thigh, the knee when necessary, and the inside of the lower leg. Grip, when needed, will become a natural reflex, and it should start at the lower leg and work up. Gripping with the lower leg

20

To be in balance the rider's body must be upright, with the shoulders open, the neck touching the back of the collar and the eyes looking forward.

In balance, over trotting poles. Ankles flexed, knees soft, hips supple.

below the lowest part of the horse's barrel and allowing the knee to remain supple gives the rider a greater feeling of security and also encourages the seat to sink deeper and further forward in the saddle. Pushing the hips forward also helps in keeping the back straight. The rider's back and loins should never get rounded in a convex to the rear; this will only stiffen the body and put the rider 'behind the movement'.

The rider should aim at a feeling of lightness in the saddle by lifting his chest. *'Ride Tall' is a very good motto for the beginner.*

The horse moves at various paces and rhythms and the rider's body must conform to this movement. No muscles must be rigid or forced.

The lower leg below the lowest part of the horse's barrel and the knee remaining supple gives the rider a greater feeling of security. This is a good lower leg position.

HANDS

Now a word about hands. It is not possible to have good 'educated' hands without a firm and independent seat, but it is possible from the beginning to put hands and arms in a position that will teach the rider to develop his hands. Softness of the elbows, suppleness of fingers and wrists are an essential to good hands, so let us try to get them sensitive to the horse's mouth from the beginning. The upper arm should hang naturally from the shoulder and when the rein is held with fingers curled towards the inside and thumb on top, the rein should be of sufficient length for the elbow to be in front of the hip. The elbow should never go behind the hip; this will stiffen the whole body.

The horse should now be walked round and the rider allowed to feel the movement of the horse's head and neck. At an ordinary walk the head swings up and down; maintain a light contact and follow this swing with soft elbows and elastic fingers and wrists, attempting to keep a straight line from the elbow to little finger down the rein to the bit. The hands should be at least the width of the bit apart. The rider's hips must swing with the horse's hips. The rider now feels the movement of the walk with his seat and his hands.

This is the beginning of good hands. When the horse is going in the required direction at the right pace the hands must follow the movement of the head and neck with a light, elastic contact. On a change of direction or a decrease of pace the indication is given to the horse by resisting the movement with one or both reins. This matter will be discussed further in the application of aids.

Softness of the elbows, suppleness of fingers and wrists are an essential to good hands.

At the walk, maintain a light contact and follow the swing of the horse's head with soft elbows and elastic fingers and wrists.

3. Balance and suppling exercises

When the rider has attained the correct position in the saddle he must then practise exercises to develop his natural balance and his muscles to keep him there. To be a competent horseman the rider must appear at ease in the saddle, but at the same time be able to apply his aids clearly, distinctly and independently of each other. To achieve this he must be in true balance without support from the reins and have complete control of his muscles.

The best way to do these exercises in the beginning is 'on the lunge' with a good instructor to help and criticise. Exercises should never be done as a drill; in fact they should be carried out light-heartedly, which in itself will help the rider to relax. Five minutes a day will make a remarkable difference to a rider's seat and general competence. From the start one should aim at the independence of each part of the body; if you are swinging one arm, make certain the other is still; if you are using one leg, make certain the other is not thrust forward and rigid or that you are forcing with your hands.

The following exercises should be done at the beginning of the ride for five minutes—first at the halt without stirrups, with the reins on the horse's neck.

Hold the pommel lightly with two fingers of each hand: then lift both thighs slightly from the saddle with knees bent; keep your back upright and feel the weight of the body on your seat bones. Repeat six times.

Now stretch down and back with your knee and up with your back; look up to the roof; then relax. Repeat six times.

Hip relaxing exercise, holding the pommel and lifting both thighs slightly away from the saddle.

Learning to 'Ride Tall'.

Stretching down and back with the knee, looking up to the roof.

Now bring the knees back to a more natural position on the saddle: circle your feet outwards to supple the ankles.

Now with the lower legs still and close to your horse's side move each hand independently; one to the right, one forward, one up, one down; do this exercise smoothly and in rhythm.

Put alternate hands behind the neck and force the elbows backwards and forwards.

Swing lower leg back and catch it with the hand, right and left alternately.

Put both hands, knuckles down, on the back of the saddle and push, forcing the chest forward and arching the back.

Muscles act by contracting and this is a natural reflex which must be overcome. All these exercises aim at extending the muscles, which also

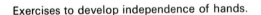

Exercises to develop independence of hands.

Suppling the knee.

Back exercise. Both hands on the back of the saddle, pushing upward and arching the back.

improve the rider's balance and at the same time help to give him confidence. They should be done daily at the halt until the rider can carry them out with confidence and ease: later they should be done at a walk and then at a trot.

If the rider is fortunate enough to have an experienced instructor who can work him on the lunge, so much the better. You need a horse that will go quietly on the circle at walk, trot and eventually canter.

WORK WITHOUT STIRRUPS

A word of warning. A great deal of damage can be done by working too long without stirrups. If the muscles get tired the rider will adopt an incorrect position to ease them. They should be done for a few minutes only each day when your horse is settled. Remember the object of the exercises: to encourage a deeper seat, to improve balance and confidence, to supple the body and limbs and make them work independently of each other. The object of the exercises is not to encourage grip, so the knee and thigh must lie passively against the saddle with the inside of the lower leg behind the girth and close to the horse's side.

USE OF STIRRUPS

Stirrup irons are on the saddle for your safety and comfort and they should be used correctly—by allowing the weight to go down towards them and not by stiffening the ankle and knee and pushing away from them. Practise this exercise *with* your stirrups as the last exercise each day, like this. Horse at the halt. Stirrup iron on the ball of your foot. Ankle flexed with the heel just lower than the toe. Knees supple. Body inclined forward with back flat. Eyes looking forward at your own height. Now raise the seat from the saddle about two inches, allowing the weight of the body to sink more into the heel. If there is any difficulty, place one hand forward on the horse's mane, but if you are truly in

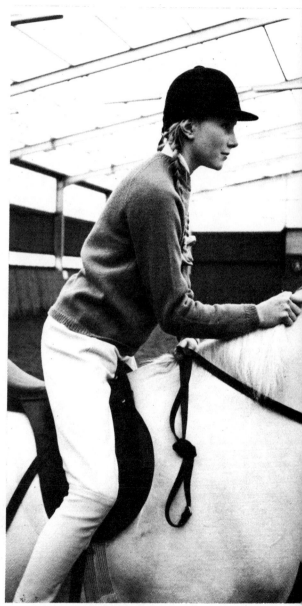

Rising trot exercises. Incline forward, back flat, eyes looking forward at your own height. Raise the seat from the saddle about two inches, allowing the weight of the body to sink more into the heel. At first you may wish to hold the horse's mane.

When you are truly in balance this rising trot exercise should be done without touching the horse's mane.

balance this exercise should be achieved without touching the reins or mane at halt and walk. This is a good preliminary to the rising trot, by the way. Make certain you feel the horse's sides with the inside of your lower leg and that the stirrup irons are kept at right angles to the horse's body.

4.   Application of the simple aids

We convey our demands to the trained horse by certain signals which we call aids. The horse must be trained to obey them, so the rider must be trained to apply these aids correctly and in harmony. The natural aids are: the legs, hands, weight of the body (through the seat) and the voice. Artificial aids are whips, spurs, martingales etc. From the beginning the rider must realise the effect the aids have on the horse's movements.

THE VOICE

The voice used softly has a quietening and soothing effect. Used sharply as a command it will teach the horse to increase pace. The voice should never be used loudly—as we have already mentioned the horse's hearing is very sensitive and it would have a frightening effect on him—and, of course, it should never be used to berate him. It should not be used at all in competition or in the show ring. In fact, its use is penalised in dressage tests.

WEIGHT

The weight of the body can be a very effective aid in changing the balance and direction of the horse. The difficulty with the novice rider

The rising trot showing the rider's centrally-placed weight.

is that, lacking a truly firm and independent seat, the weight is used in such a way that it very often hinders the horse rather than aids him. The novice rider should be taught to keep his weight even on both seat bones and to follow the movements of his horse by using his weight in the direction required, without exaggerated movement of the upper body. The more advanced rider will shift the balance of his weight correctly to assist his aids in training a young horse, and as the education of horse and rider reaches a high standard extra pressure on one stirrup will be sufficient indication.

LEGS

The rider's legs have two important functions. Firstly, acting with equal force close to the girth they create and maintain impulsion; and, secondly, they control the hindquarters. By using one leg with greater force behind the girth the hindquarters of a trained horse can be moved laterally. The legs should be used lightly until more force is required, and to do this it is important that the inside of the leg remains in light contact with the horse's side; it must stay passive until an aid is applied. The continued flap, flap, flap of a rider's legs against his horse's sides only results in deadening this sensitive area, with the result that harder kicking is needed. As the rider improves he should carry a switch or schooling whip about three feet long. A touch with this whip behind the rider's leg to reinforce a light leg aid will very soon produce a horse that is sensitive to the slightest indication.

HANDS

We have already said in chapter 1 that the first step to good hands is to acquire a firm and independent seat. Finesse in the application of the aids is the next stage. Good hands are normally passive, the movement conforming to the movement of the horse's head. They should rarely act (except in a movement such as a half-halt). They resist to decrease pace. They yield to increase pace or at the completion of a downward transition. The hands should never pull, which is why it is most important for the rider to develop the correct reflexes, to sit in a position of resistance when necessary and to always have a correct length of rein.

The amount of resistance of the hand must never be more than the resistance of the horse, and should cease instantly when the horse's resistance ceases. Most riders use their hands too much and their legs not enough. If a rider has good hands in a good position they are rarely noticed. Your eye will be directed to 'busy' hands, which are bad hands.

In the early stages the rider must be told that the hands must never be in opposition to the legs. When the legs ask for forward movement the hands must yield, ideally maintaining a light elastic contact by the suppleness of fingers and wrists and the softness of the elbows.

The type of rein used has an effect on hands. The reins should be broad and non-slip, so that the fingers and thumb can close on them firmly when resisting; also in the early stages of learning to ride the mildest snaffle bit compatible with control is essential.

HARMONY OF THE AIDS

The hands, through the medium of the reins, control and develop the impulsion created by the rider's legs. The horse should therefore be pushed towards the bit, and not the bit pulled back by the rider's hand towards the horse.

Let's take the simple example of decreasing pace from a walk to the halt, a transition that is often done badly. We have said that at the walk the rider must follow the swing of the head with a light contact, keeping in rhythm with hand and body. Now to decrease pace his hand must resist the movement, but to resist successfully the first action must come from a firm base, i.e. the body. The back is arched and the hips pushed towards the hands; the hands decrease their movement, then stop. The

41

Most riders use their hands too much. This is a transition ot pace from walk to halt, showing the rider using tactful hands and her own back to help a smooth transition. There is a little resistance in the horse's mouth here.

Another transition to halt showing an insecure seat and rough hands . . .

horse stops—straight, with a steady head carriage and no resistance, because the hindquarters have been made to assist in the halt, acting as the break, which is their proper function when decreasing pace. This is a fundamental in the application of the aids. The seat, and when necessary the legs, must always be used before the hand whether increasing or decreasing pace.

DIAGONAL AID

The same principle applies when changing direction right or left. The rider must realise that the horse must always look in the direction he is going. Let us say we wish to turn to the right. With the legs asking the horse to go forward, the right hand is carried outwards; this leads the

. . . and here the lower leg has gone forward and the reins are too long. The seat is weak and the back is stiff.

horse's nose to the right and he follows it in a soft turn. This is called the Open Rein. As the rider becomes more adept he learns to produce this effect without carrying out his hand. If the inside hand, in this case the right, produces the bend, the outside must work in harmony by allowing the bend, and easing a little without losing contact. The horse's hind feet must follow in the track of his forefeet, so the rider's outside leg, the left in this case, is drawn a little behind the girth to control the quarters; the inside leg is still on the girth to maintain forward movement. This is called the Diagonal Aid, where each hand and each leg have a different task but work in harmony. This aid is used throughout equitation. It is the emphasis with which it is used that produces an infinite variety of effects.

Care must be taken that right and left rein aids and right and left leg

A simple diagonal aid to the left, the horse looking in the direction in which he is going.

aids do not work in opposition to each other; if the right rein asks for bend, the left must yield to allow it; it must also regulate the amount of bend and control the pace. If the right leg acts to produce a movement of the quarters, the left leg at first yields and then resists to regulate the movement.

Study and practice is essential if the aids are to be applied with tact and finesse. But the first thing to remember and practise is: *the seat and legs initiate a movement, the hands, through the medium of the reins, guide and control it*. Only by riding a reasonably well-trained horse can the novice rider learn to feel the effects of the aids. It just isn't feasible to expect untrained riders to ride effectively on 'green' horses.

5. Rider's position at walk and trot

THE WALK

The walk is a calm, easy pace with a four-time beat, and the rider learns to sit in rhythm and apply the aids to: Advance straight forward; Halt; Turn and Circle. This work must be done accurately, riding to markers, not just going forward without a sense of direction.

Look at your marker before turning, and then ride squarely towards it. Where your eyes look is important. Looking down affects the back and will cause rounded shoulders and slack loins, making the seat sloppy and unstable. By looking forward, always at your own height, your balance is improved and your back and loins kept erect. Overcome the natural tendency to lean forward. All influence of the seat is lost when this happens, for by leaning forward you weight the hands and legs and your aids cannot be applied effectively. By leaning forward you also weaken the seat and put more weight on the horse's forehand, making it more difficult to control him.

By sitting upright with more weight on the seat you give freedom of action to the hands and legs. Working at the walk you will be able to concentrate quite easily on: position, application of aids and accuracy of movement. Combined with balance exercises at the halt, your balance, muscle control and confidence will develop rapidly. Also at the walk you should practise lengthening the reins by allowing them to slide quietly through the fingers, and then just as quietly take them up again to the

A walk is a calm, easy pace with a four-time beat. This rider shows a good position at the walk.

Look at your marker when turning, then ride squarely towards it.

Riding down the centre line, A to C.

correct length. This exercise helps to develop independence of the hands and tactful handling of the reins.

THE TROT

Only when the beginner can carry out the work just dealt with at halt and walk with confidence should the trot be attempted. A reasonable balance at halt and walk should have been achieved and thigh muscles stretched and strengthened by this time. Also before starting to trot the balance exercise of rising at the halt with stirrups should again be practised until the rider can do this exercise in balance without holding the mane.

The best way to get the 'feel' of the trot is to be put on 'the lunge' with a quiet horse and experienced instructor, the rider sitting upright and holding the saddle. If this isn't possible the trot should be practised in an enclosed space, the rider holding the reins in one hand and the pommel (two fingers hooked lightly—under it) with the other.

SITTING TROT

To be secure it is a good idea to tie the stirrups to the girth for the first two or three attempts. It allows them to hang straight but stops excessive movement of the lower leg. The lower leg position governs very much the upper part of the body and also helps in the security of the seat. Make certain, therefore, that the lower leg is in the correct position under the rider's shoulder (this will bring it just behind the perpendicular); that the heel is lower than the toe, to tension the calf muscles; and that the inside of the calf is close to the horse's side. Keep the knee supple and allow it to come away from the saddle a little at first. To begin the trot, tension the calf muscles, squeezing in with them sharply, at the same time easing the rein. Hold yourself in the saddle with the fingers of the right hand in the pommel; keep the body upright and the eyes looking forward. After a few strides return to a walk by applying the same aid as from walk to halt. The trot is a pace of two-time with the horse springing

Holding the saddle for the sitting trot exercise.

alternately from one pair of diagonals to the other. Try to count this beat with the seat firmly in the saddle on each actual beat.

RISING TROT

Having got the feel of the sitting trot, it is easier to try the rising trot until the muscles are further developed. In the rising trot the body is inclined slightly forward and the rider lets himself be pushed up on one beat, allowing the seat to come down into the saddle on the next beat. Exactly as practised in the balance exercise, reins are in the left hand and the right hand holds the mane. Apply the legs and ease the hand, and when your horse is trotting commence rising. Once the rhythm is achieved take a rein in each hand and practise rising without any increased tension on the reins. This is most important—so many riders pull themselves forward by the reins. In trot, the horse's head is comparatively still; therefore the hands must remain still with the same light, unvarying contact.

To do the rising trot in balance and maintain the influence of the seat, the rider must ensure that the lower leg position is correctly against the curve of the horse's side, the weight of the body lowering the heel, the knee supple and close to the saddle but without squeezing. The movement forward and upward must come from the hips, and the shoulders go forward with the hips, with the seat coming firmly into the saddle on each alternate beat. The eyes as always looking forward. Too many people rise by pinching with the knee and bending the body forward; this pushes the seat to the rear, and the all-important influence of the seat is lost.

The sitting trot should only be used at this stage when increasing or decreasing pace. Until the rider's suppleness improves and the thigh muscles are developed it is very tiring and can do positive harm to the rider's position and to the pace of the horse. This will be discussed in a later chapter.

In the rising trot the body is inclined slightly forward and the rider lets himself be pushed up on one beat, allowing the seat to come down into the saddle on the next beat.

6. More active riding

WORK AT THE TROT

The rider must now practise in rising trot all the exercises he did at the walk. The first are the increase of pace to trot and the decrease to walk. When both legs are applied and the hand eased, the horse should advance actively into trot: the schooling whip should be used lightly to reinforce the leg aid if the response is not immediate. When the correct pace is achieved, commence rising; the legs should be passive but ready to sustain the pace.

To reduce pace from trot to walk the rider prepares his horse by sitting, then straightens his back and closes the legs very slightly; the hand then resists the movement until the horse walks. The horse will lower his haunches slightly and the head carriage will be steady; the rider's hand will take up the rhythm of the walk. Both these exercises have an important bearing on all transitions and should be practised with tact until they are perfect.

All turns, inclines and changes of direction should be executed accurately but softly, with the horse bent on the line of movement and the hind feet following in the track of the forefeet. The rider's inside leg must maintain impulsion. Circles should be large and accurate, a perfect twenty-metre circle being the aim, and not a flat-sided, nebulous figure.

THE DIAGONALS

We have said the trot is a pace of diagonals with the rider sitting on one diagonal and rising on the other. The rider should learn to change the diagonal by an extra bump in the saddle. This is soon learned with a little practice. If the rider stays on the same diagonal, the horse will become stiff and awkward on the other diagonal. Regular changing ensures that he trots evenly on both. In the riding school or manège it is customary to change the diagonal when changing the rein. When working in the riding school—or outside for that matter—the rider aims at a steady, even rhythm in his ordinary trot, a pace of about seven miles an hour, active but calm. This is the basis of schooling and of developing good paces. As soon as the rider is reasonably confident and capable of maintaining the seat and controlling his horse at walk and trot in the manège, some slow work across natural country should be encouraged, on a quiet horse and in company with an experienced horseman. Work up and down hills over gently undulating ground helps to develop the rider's balance, and to anticipate movements. This natural bringing together of the horse and rider's equilibrium brings ease and grace to the position, although one must still be very conscious of faults and always ready to give rein when the horse asks for it.

But remember, to enjoy riding in the open to its fullest one must become competent first in the riding school. This applies to horse or rider, and if these early lessons are worked at conscientiously a happy combination can be produced.

SITTING TROT

The sitting trot is an extremely valuable exercise for the rider, and is indispensable in schooling at a later stage. It must not be attempted too soon or for too long periods. The rider must learn to sit without clutching with the knee and thigh, so the first four lessons should be aimed at keeping the body erect with shoulders and heels back. Hold the saddle

Work in the open—uphill, and downhill, rider's body remaining in balance in each case, giving freedom to the horse's hindquarters.

with the right hand and reins with the left, as in the first lesson. This keeps the hips forward towards the front of the saddle and helps to maintain an erect body which improves the balance. A slow jog is all that is necessary to begin, until the rider can sit with a good posture comfortably. When the horse relaxes his back and neck muscles, the rider will have relaxed. The sitting trot is perfected by keeping a straight back and supple loin with the weight of the rider firmly on the seat bones; a supple knee and ankle allows the weight of the rider's legs to go down to the stirrup irons. This feeling of security which is felt when holding the saddle will soon be achieved for short periods when letting go of the saddle. If the rider loses balance or his seat slips to the rear, he should immediately hold the saddle again.

The sitting trot without stirrups when done correctly is a fine balance and suppling exercise, but it must only be done for short periods; otherwise muscles become tired, and in attempting to save them the rider develops an incorrect, stiff position.

Eventually, all balance exercises that are practised at halt and walk should be carried out at the trot.

7. Faster paces

TROTTING POLES

Before training starts at any faster pace I believe a certain amount of work should be done over poles on the ground. It helps to improve the balance and to develop the right muscles. If a horse becomes unbalanced the reaction of the novice horseman is to throw the body back and pull with the hands; the opposite must be learned, that is to keep the weight forward and allow freedom to the head and neck so that the horse may recover his own balance. One of the great difficulties for the horse is to learn to carry the weight of the rider, and the educated rider will help him by staying in balance under all circumstances.

A single heavy pole on the ground at this stage will begin a series of valuable lessons for both horse and rider. Walking over the pole teaches the rider to stay in balance by inclining the body slightly forward as the horse steps over it; the rider also 'feels' the stretching of the head and neck, which he follows with a soft elbow and supple fingers and wrists. From the horse's point of view, it teaches him to respect the pole without being afraid of it. These are also valuable first lessons in jumping.

Work over trotting poles helps to improve balance and develop the right muscles.
The rider is in balance. She has no contact here—a fault on the right side.

Still at the walk, a second pole should be introduced, between four and a half to five and a half feet apart, depending on the horse's natural stride. Again quietly walk over these with the weight slightly forward and hands following.

Then try the two rails in rising trot; a slow rhythm should be second nature by now. The rising trot carries the rider's body naturally forward; the horse trots over the two poles, and the only difference in the 'feel' is that the swing of the horse's back is accentuated; the rhythm remains the same. With patience and practice six poles may be negotiated, the rider still in rising trot, working from both directions and on both reins. Constant attention should be paid to the rider's position, the most important points being the softness of the knee and ankle acting as buffers; the rider looking ahead and keeping the back flat; the hand maintaining a light and even contact.

The most important part of the jump is the approach, and these exercises over trotting poles also teach the horse to come in straight, to adjust his balance, relax the back and neck muscles and to engage his hocks. When the time comes for the young rider to jump, early lessons will be made much easier by this calm approach. Work over the trotting poles may be practised with and without reins. Sitting trot must only be tried when the rider is strong enough and the horse really swings his back; then it may be done with and without stirrups.

THE CANTER

The canter appears to the novice as an exciting and invigorating pace, with the result that most new riders attempt to canter too soon—before their seat has been reasonably established at walk and trot.

The canter is a pace of three-time, and to enable a horse to turn quickly and safely he should canter with the inside foreleg leading followed by the inside hindleg. In the trot we had a two-time rhythm and a still head carriage: in the canter we have a three-time rhythm, a little increase in speed, and the horse swinging his head. This is a rocking thythm and to maintain balance the seat must synchronise with this motion. It is most important first to allow the horse to swing his head, second to keep the body upright and third to keep the knees supple and bent so that the weight of the body is on the seat bones and not pushed down to the ball of the foot with a stiff knee; this last natural reflex action only pushes the seat on the back of the saddle, and must be overcome from the start.

At first, hold the saddle with one hand and a fairly short rein in the other, preferably the inside hand. To strike off, ask your horse to canter either on a circle or out of a corner; this should position him correctly for the inside lead. To do this from a sitting trot apply both legs, inside leg on the girth, outside leg behind the girth. Keeping the body upright and looking forward as your horse strikes off, your bridle hand goes forward and the hand holding the saddle pulls the pelvis towards the front.

POSITION AT CANTER

To allow the back and loins to flex in rhythm with the undulating motion, the back must be stretched upright and the heels kept below the shoulders. Rounding the back in a mistaken attempt to be supple only increases the weight on the rider's loins and causes stiffness. When the rider has acquired sufficient suppleness, the head and shoulders should appear to be still and staying in line with the heels; the swing takes place at the waist. Riders who swing their shoulders forward at each stride are stiff in the waist and knee and will not be able to apply an accurate aid in canter.

This shows a good position at the canter. The young rider has a supple hip, knee and ankle. The seat is deep, body erect, eyes looking forward. Correct length of rein and light contact.

Another canter shot. Here the reins are too long and the seat is slipping a little to the rear.

TRANSITION CANTER TO TROT

The principle has been explained earlier but in this transition the effective use of the back will be felt more by the rider. The back muscles are braced slightly, the seat pushed to the front, the legs remain close to the horse's sides; the hand resists the movement and the horse decreases pace in a balanced manner with his hocks underneath him; the head carriage is steady.

Cantering should be practised only for very short periods to begin with. Practise in the transitions—trot to canter; canter to trot, first holding the saddle, and later with a rein in each hand—will quickly teach the rider to co-ordinate his hands and body to the changing rhythm.

Too many riders hang on to their horse's head when cantering. The horse must be allowed to carry himself; pulling on the reins only encourages the horse to depend on this unnecessary support, and the more the rider hangs on, the more the horse will lean. Develop the seat independently of the reins. Five minutes work on the lunge twice a week is invaluable if one wishes to acquire this ideal.

LENGTH OF STIRRUP

As the rider's muscles develop and the seat deepens it will be found possible to lengthen the stirrups by two or more holes when working on the flat at the basic paces. This must be done with care; it allows greater use of the legs in applying the aids, but if done too soon it will cause the rider to tip forward and weaken the seat.

On the other hand, the rider may shorten the stirrups preparatory to jumping. If shortened too much the seat will be pushed to the rear, causing insecurity and loss of influence.

Basically, the seat must be developed with a length of stirrup that allows the rider to carry out all normal activities with maximum comfort and control. When this seat is achieved the rider may lengthen a little for school work or shorten for jumping and cross-country work.

A good length of stirrup for all normal activities.

In the school we ask our horse to obey delicately applied aids. Across country, as in hunting, we move faster and for much longer periods. We must therefore ride lightly, saving our horse as much as possible, so the stirrup is shortened, enabling the rider to carry his weight further forward and leaving the loins and propelling muscles free to carry out their tasks. You will see the extremes of stirrup length typified in the dressage rider at one end of the scale and flat race jockey at the other.

8. First steps in jumping

To progress from our trotting poles to jumping small fences is but a small step provided the work over poles has been thorough. The rider should now shorten his leathers by one or two holes; this gives greater mechanical advantage without materially altering the seat.

A pole about 18″ to 2′ high should now be placed about nine to ten feet away from the last trotting pole. There should be no exaggerated movement by the rider over this small jump. The trotting poles have taught him to sit in balance with shoulders just in front of the hips, seat bones in the saddle, with a little more of his weight on the knee and thigh and down to the stirrup iron: the heel sinks a little, thereby tightening the calf muscles.

As the horse takes off, the angle between body and thigh closes, the hand follows the movement of horse's head and neck, fingers opening slightly. The minimum of movement to maintain balance is all that is required. The legs remain close to the horse's side with the stirrup leathers vertical and the rider's seat close to the saddle.

As fences get bigger and wider, the parabola of the leap becomes greater. Greater effort is required by the rider to keep in balance; the body goes further forward, the seat leaves the saddle more, but the principle of minimum movement remains.

The rider should then begin to take a more active part in the approach and take-off by using his legs quietly in rhythm with the stride when trotting in. There should be no sudden thump in the ribs on take-off. The horse should be encouraged forward and not punished forward. The

Jumping a small fence. Here two cavaletti are used. The body position is good, but the hands are heavy, restricting the freedom of the horse's head and neck . . .

. . . and in this picture the elbows are stiff and sticking out and the rider is standing in his stirrups.

Here the hands are much more sensitive and the body position correct with the rider looking forward. A good jump.

correct use of the leg on the approach is most important, and few riders do it well.

MORE ACTIVE JUMPING

Our next step is to give the rider more 'feel' over the small fence. Build it into a parallel two feet high and two feet apart. Now the horse rounds his back more; there is a little more movement to the rider's hand as the neck stretches and the body goes further forward. Great attention must still be paid to the rider's performance on the flat—he must still turn correctly before the approach, he must ride forward on a straight line on landing and turn again correctly. Ideally the trotting poles and small fence should be placed on the centre line so that a continual change of rein is possible.

Now we progress to more participation by the rider. Another fence of the same height and width is placed 18 feet from the first parallel, giving one canter stride. Concentrate now on use of leg rhythm between fences; hands quiet, body in balance.

Place another fence 21 feet further on, then another 33 feet from this, giving two strides. There are many possible combinations, but don't try to surprise your horse; just keep horse and rider thinking.

The rider should count the strides between fences and the number of pressures of the lower leg that are needed. Seat bones must come back into the saddle between fences. Hands must be steady and completely independent of the body and legs, maintaining their light contact. If something goes wrong and balance is lost, the hands allow the rein to slip through the fingers. *Remember, your hands belong to your horse's mouth.*

Fences must remain small until horse and rider can negotiate various distances smoothly and in perfect harmony. They may be raised gradually up to 3 feet high and 4 feet spread, but make certain they look solid and are firm on their stands—a flimsy schooling fence can cause much harm.

At this stage the rider will begin to develop an eye for distance; this is

Cavaletti work. This is a good layout at a progressive school.

The most important part of a jump—the approach. This is a good position; seat in the saddle, rider looking forward . . .

the beginning of being able to *see* your stride; *adjusting* the stride is another and more difficult matter, and is a long way off yet.

JUMPING A COURSE

Up to now the rider's role on the approach has been a comparatively passive one, the cavaletti poles doing the work for him. Our next stage is to get horse and rider going quietly round a simple course with smooth, easy changes of direction. Fences must remain small, with emphasis on spread rather than height. The pace between fences must be the trot, with one or two canter strides into each fence, then back to trot.

No horse should be ridden round even the simplest course until he is calm and readily obedient to the aids. So work on the flat must always be a preliminary to jumping, until the horse learns to change direction calmly and smoothly between fences, first at a trot then later at canter

Topping the fence. Body and hands correct, but the lower leg has slipped back a little . . .

Landing. The rider's hands give complete freedom to head and neck, but maintain light contact. A good position, although the rider's back has become slightly rounded.

and gallop, with his body always bent on the line of movement. He must learn to lengthen and shorten his stride with a steady head carriage and always remaining nicely 'on the bit'.

The most important phase of the jump is the approach, the skill with which the horse is ridden up to the point of take-off. Now that the trotting poles have been removed and the rider is beginning to ride a small course, he must, as we have said, begin to play a more active part on the approach. The good horseman remains quietly in balance with his shoulders in front of his hips but his seat bones in the saddle, lower leg close to his horse's sides, the hands maintaining a light contact throughout. The rider's task is to bring his horse to the point of take-off in balance, at the right speed, and with sufficient impulsion to clear the fence. During the last few strides there is often a moment when the rider contracts his fingers and elbows and allows his legs to go limp, particularly when the approach appears to be wrong. Exactly the opposite reaction is required; the seat should be firmly in the saddle, the lower leg being used as a pushing aid working in rhythm with the stride, the approach being made with mounting impulsion.

ADJUSTING THE STRIDE

As the rider gains experience he will begin to 'see his stride', judge whether he is going to meet his fence rightly or wrongly, and remedy the situation by either lengthening or shortening the stride. Any alteration in stride must be done smoothly and as far away from the fence as possible.

A great deal can be learnt by the use of a distance rail; place a cavaletti two, three or more strides away from a larger fence. This distance rail gives horse and rider confidence and helps to develop the rider's eye. It can be used with success over all types of fences.

Interfere as little as possible on the approach. Provided your horse is well balanced and has the requisite impulsion he will jump most fences up to four feet high (depending on his natural ability and state of

74

A good example of a firm, independent seat, with rider in balance looking forward and using light hands.

Another good position. This youngster's body is nicely in balance with her seat close to the saddle. Hands light, but maintaining contact.

training) without being 'placed'.

RIDING ACROSS COUNTRY

I have dealt here only with jumping in its early stages in manège or
school. In jumping solid obstacles across country the principles remain
the same. Accurate and patient work in the school will produce bold
but calm cross-country riders. Competence produces courage—any
apprehension or hesitancy on the part of the rider will be quickly
transmitted to the horse with unhappy results. Most horses are keener
when being ridden in the open or in company, so the rider must always
try to keep his mount between hand and leg, first at the trot, then slow
canter, gradually going forward to the gallop; but obedience must come
at the slow paces first.

THE GALLOP

The gallop has a four-time rhythm. It is achieved by increasing the
canter, the horse stretching his stride until each foot comes to the ground
one after the other. There is a moment at the end of each stride where
all four feet are off the ground; this is called 'the period of suspension'.
As in the canter a horse should gallop with the inside foreleg leading.

At this pace with a free going horse the rider's body should be further
forward with the seat bones just clear of the saddle, allowing complete
freedom to the horse's back and loins.

The stirrup leathers must remain vertical, the rider being in balance
by virtue of the forward position of the shoulder and the use of the ankle
and knee as shock absorbers, and not by hanging on to the horse's mouth.

The ability to maintain a uniform pace at the gallop, particularly
when riding across undulating or broken ground, is a good test of the
skill and tact with which the rider harmonises the use of hand and leg.

To gallop a 'sticky' horse the seat bones must be firmly pushing in the
saddle, so that the action of the rider's legs is unimpeded by the weight
of the body.

Gallop; 1st beat.   This shows a good position at the gallop. The seat is out of the saddle, shoulders forward but not in front of the knees.

Gallop; between 2nd and 3rd beat.   Here the heel is well sunk (slightly more than in the previous picture), enabling calf muscles to tension properly.

Gallop; 3rd beat.   The rider is still in a good position, although the hands have moved up a little too high.

Gallop; 4th beat.   A good position again, with correct light contact.

9. Improving your horse

It has been estimated that the horse in his natural state carries three-quarters of his weight on his forelegs. If we place a rider on his back, this will increase the weight on the forelegs and also upset his natural balance. To make our horse into a light and pleasant ride this weight must be brought more to the rear, that is on to the hind-quarters. To do this, the horse must learn by exercises to develop activity in the hip, stifle and hock joints so that the quarters are lowered and the hocks come further under the body. This obviously will lighten the forehand and improve the balance. This can only be done by developing the right muscles with progressive exercises, mainly at walk and trot, over a period of time. Muscle is like a piece of elastic; it works by contraction, and also like a piece of elastic the more you stretch it the farther it will contract. So we must first teach our horse to extend the right muscles so that they may be developed to maximum strength and elasticity.

The rider's weight must be as close to the withers as possible, so that the green horse will be encouraged to carry this weight correctly, that is by rounding his back and extending his neck. This is the beginning of developing the dorsal muscles of the neck, the suppling of the loins and the engagement of the hocks. Before the horse can carry himself and his rider in balance he must first be allowed to move in an extended attitude. With the head lowered and neck extended his shoulders will begin to move freely and the hocks will become further engaged under

Typical attitude of a young horse, with his weight mainly on the forehand and neck extended. Compare this with the pictures overleaf, a horse more advanced in training.

the body. Our training must be methodical and it is a combination of work in the open over natural country, and in the school or manège.

IN THE OPEN

Over natural undulating country or gentle hills the horse must be worked on straight lines. Working on a longish rein he will extend the neck, move in a relaxed manner with a swing to his back; first at the walk and then in trot. An even pace must be maintained, the rider keeping his weight forward and legs close to the horse's sides. The horse will not relax unless he is calm; therefore he must go calmly at the walk before he is allowed to trot. This will take at least two weeks with a young horse.

The Walk; 1st beat.

The Walk; 2nd beat.

This sequence shows a good walk, active but calm. The walk is a pace of four-time in which the horse lifts each foot up and puts it down separately. Starting with a hind leg the sequence is this: 1. Near hind. 2. Near fore. 3. Off hind. 4. Off fore. The horse should walk with a swing to his back

The Walk; 3rd beat.

and the natural movement of the head should not be impeded by the rider's hands. The pictures show a 'free' walk on a long rein. Other type of walks that are recognised are: the 'ordinary' walk, the 'collected' walk and the 'extended' walk.

The Walk; 4th beat.

The Trot; rider on left diagonal. The trot is a pace of two-time on alternate diagonals (the near fore and off hind is the left diagonal, and the off fore and near hind is the right). In this picture the rider is riding on the left diagonal with her seat in the saddle as the left diagonal is on the ground. The diagonals should be changed regularly when riding, or the horse becomes stiff and awkward on the diagonal not used.

During this time the young horse will gain confidence in his rider, which helps him to relax. At this pace there is no risk of damage to limbs or to the mouth. He must be allowed freedom of the head and neck and encouraged to walk with long, energetic strides.

84

The Trot; period of suspension. In the trot the horse should spring from one diagonal to the other. Here you see the moment of suspension between diagonals, when all the feet are off the ground.

The Trot; with some extension. The recognised trots are: 'ordinary', 'collected' and 'extended' trot. This picture illustrates some extension, in which the rhythm is kept but the pace covers more ground.

The Canter; 1st beat.

The canter is a pace of three-time. For example, with the off fore leading, the footfalls are these: 1. Near hind. 2. Near fore and off hind together—the left diagonal.

The Canter; 2nd beat.

The Canter; 3rd beat.

3. Off fore.
Then a moment of suspension, when all feet are off the ground.

The Canter; period of suspension.

IN THE SCHOOL

Work in the school also goes ahead with progressive exercises, but the rider must insist on obedience in the easy, simple things. The horse must learn to stand quietly and still whilst bit, reins, girth or stirrups are adjusted. After the rider has mounted, the horse should be made to stand still for a further minute; this overcomes any anticipatory fidgeting. All work in the school should be calm and methodical, the rider having clearly in his mind the object of each lesson, and how he is going to achieve it. Lessons in the school should never be too long; with a young horse twenty minutes to half-an-hour after his work outside is ample. This depends entirely on the horse's temperament, but nothing will be gained unless the horse is calm. What is the aim in our school work?

(1) Calmness and confidence.
(2) To teach the horse to go freely forward from the leg on to the bit.
(3) To be obedient to hand and leg.
(4) To improve his paces.
(5) To develop his muscles so that he can carry himself and the weight of his rider in a balanced manner.
(6) To be supple, laterally and longitudinally.
(7) *To go straight.*

We want our horse to be a happy, amiable ride and easy to control at all paces. No force, compulsion or punishment must be employed in his schooling. The saddlery we use is of the simplest—a well-fitting jointed snaffle and on most horses a dropped nose band carefully fitted. Comfort is vital—a good central-position saddle and a supple girth. A nylon girth is comparatively cheap and very good.

A neck strap to hold on to when outside, for use up hills or over rough ground, will save your horse's mouth. In the school the rider should carry a schooling whip sufficiently long and flexible to be used to reinforce a leg aid without taking the hand from the rein. It will normally be carried in the inside hand and lie passively across the thigh. It should be used lightly and quickly behind the rider's leg when the response to an aid is not sufficiently active. A sluggish response may be due to laziness or weakness—the two must not be confused. If a horse has been trained to obey the whip on the lunge he will understand its use when mounted, and provided it is used sparingly he will obey it without fearing it.

THE PACES

In all school movements the rider must aim to develop the purity and regularity of the basic paces. He must study the footfalls of each pace and must learn to feel when the pace is right and when the rhythm is even. To help the horse in the early stages all turns must be soft and easy, circles large, with the hind feet following in the track of the forefeet. Transitions must not be abrupt. The horse should move forward smoothly but actively from the leg; decrease of pace must be prepared for and made gradually, to allow the horse to adjust his balance and engage his hocks with lowered quarters.

CONCLUSION

If you wish to learn to ride competently, and eventually own your own horse, go to the nearest good riding school. If you are in doubt about a school write to the British Horse Society. The B.H.S. keeps an up-to-date list of approved riding schools and will advise you of the best one in your area. If you genuinely wish to become a *good* horseman, not only must you perfect your seat and the proper application of the aids, but you must also study the theory of riding—all under proper instruction.

This is essential if you want to learn to ride with 'feel' and a knowledge of why we ask our horse to carry out certain movements and exercises.

By this means you will progress to the second stage of equitation, which is to carry out more advanced movements on a trained horse and also to teach a young horse basic schooling, both on the flat and over fences, in the manège and across country.

10. Jumping—a pictorial analysis

Not a classic position, but there is no interference with the horse's mouth here. The rider's toe is down, causing the lower leg to slip back with a consequent loss of strength in seat.

In balance and with a light hand. The martingale arrangement is not to everyone's taste.

The hands allow freedom of head and neck. This young rider's toe has dropped and foot slipped home in the stirrup iron, which must weaken the rider's seat.

A good seat. No interference from rider. The right hand is pushed up the horse's neck, a habit learnt when the horse was young and difficult to break.

Rider's back and knee stiff; ankle locked. The whole body is out of balance, but the hands are good, giving freedom to neck extension.